Dreams

and

Desires

Jay M

ISBN: 1722095016
ISBN-13: 978-1722095017

DEDICATION

I would like to dedicate this to everyone who has been in and out of my life and the impacts they have made to create me into the individual I am today.

So, I would like to start off by saying that this book is not quite a poetry book, but in a way it is. Within this text you will find a conglomeration of various excerpts from writings in my journal that I have accumulated over an extensive amount of time.

I have chosen to put some of my favourite writings into this book in no specific order. You can find everything from journal entries, to brief philosophical thoughts, but mostly poems. I am writing this book in order to inspire and provoke thought within others; hopefully through my own thoughts. I believe we learn best by viewing other's perspectives. This is not quite my story, but simultaneously in some aspects it is... I hope you enjoy this book and relate to it in some sort of way.

I would like to also add that some of these writings may seem nonsensical and just silly poems (especially the love ones). But I encourage you to find a deeper meaning to what is within the text. I do not expect that everything you come across will make sense. That could be because you're not meant to make sense of it; where as someone else is. That's okay! That's the beauty in art.

Thank you,

J.M

As I wander alone walking through the streets on a
cool autumn afternoon,

Death whispers tempting promises in my ear.

I think about a place without pain or sadness and
one with only love and happiness,

A place that's unreal...

A distant utopia that can only live in my mind

For where I live, your nightmares feed off your tears
and blood;

I live in a place where happy endings are a distant
thought, a distant fantasy...

Something that one can only hope for but will never

get.

Death is the answer to pain, but pain is the answer to death...

But with life, death is guaranteed... So isn't pain inevitable?

There is no right answer.

There is no right life.

So all one can do is live...

#2

Some days...

Some days I want to slit my wrists in a bathtub and drown on my own blood.

Some days I want to sing and shout while dancing in the rain.

Some days I want to choke back on the barrel of a .44 and let an explosion go off in my brain.

Some days I want to hug my mother and father and let them know how much I care,

Some days I want to wrap a rope around my throat and gargle on my own spit.

Some days I want to walk down the shore of a beach with the sun washing over my skin as I smile with warmth in my heart...

Some days I stand between the crossroads of heaven and hell not knowing which path I'll go down.

#3

I walk the empty streets with an empty feeling in my
heart.

The moon stares down on me with its warm tender
glow,

The rain clicks across the drainpipes and streams
along the empty roadsides running places unknown.

Every step I take feels heavier than the last with my
thoughts weighing me down;

The silence slows my steps with my heart beat and
within a few moments I'm taking in the sights with
great intrigue.

An owl hoo's and the rain clicks,

The wind howls and the trees rustle,

I look up and the sky is strewn with stars that twinkle like gems.

The breeze wipes the tears from my eyes and replaces it with a smile,

I take a deep breath in and the cool refreshing air fills my lungs and washes out the pain with a soft exhale.

The night time takes my frustration and worries and replaces them with comfort;

When I get back, my home welcomes me with a warm embrace.

#4

Loneliness is filling my mind.

I never feel paid attention to or cared about;

Loneliness filling my heart.

I am never kept as a friend for more than a year;

Loneliness filling my arms and legs.

I always feel like I can't do anything right without
fucking up;

Loneliness fills my entire body.

Loneliness weighs down my muscles and bones,

Now I am in the fetal position and I'm crying.

Loneliness consumes my entire soul.

#5

Faces all stone like sculptures,

They all stare at me like vultures;

Wanting to cut me open and eat me inside out.

Hatred in their icy black hearts,

Staring through cold calculating eyes they watch my
every move.

Every day they strip me of my dignity bit by bit;

Bit by bit till there's nothing left but the shell of a
scared little boy.

Not caring if I cry,

Not caring if I'm lonely,

Maybe they don't like to hear me breathe...

No way to fight back.

#6

My special sweet...

I hold you so fond in my memories that no one will
ever beat.

With hair that smelt of bubble-gum,

And lips that taste of cotton candy;

You felt as soft as marsh-mellows,

And as warm as hot chocolate on a winter's day.

You melted my heart like caramel,

But sadly...

Our love has become stale.

It crumbles at my feet,

And now I get no sweetness to treat my bitter heart.

#7

Name

    after name,

        after name,

Face

    after face,

        after face,

It   never   ends.

It also never starts...

It also ends.

I begin to believe I'm no good.

Failure is the greatest predecessor to ambition,

If you let it that is...

Some let failure stop them like a train thrashing against their body at 100mph.

But reality is...

They let the illusion of failure keep them on their knees,

But when you begin to realize that it's the beginning of what's to come, and that it's a mere stepping stone;

You can truly begin to search within yourself the meaning of succession.

Because what is good without bad?

What is strong without weak?

What is smart without stupidity?

One can only come to realize once they are able to delineate that contrast.

Just a thought:

The worst kind of person is one with a weak sense of
empathy,

The type that lacks encouragement entwined with
empowerment.

#9

I travel on a boat in a sea of euphoria,

My spirit feels free, my mind wraps its arms around
me in a soft tender caress.

I take a deep breath;

The waves continue to rock as I travel on the infinite
sea of peace.

I acknowledge the way my chest pumps as I take my
breathes.

I acknowledge my hands folded in my lap.

I acknowledge my entire being and everything
around it.

I feel myself beginning to melt into the floor,

I hear someone call my name in the distance.

I snap back into reality like a whip cracked over my
conscious,

And it's back to life...

Just a thought:

Meditation is the key to true happiness, when you are able to embrace a state of mindfulness. A state in which you are living in your own headspace, whilst acknowledging the area around you. This state of mindfulness, not only enables you to escape the dreads and horrors of the real world, but you are also capable of having great epiphanies that only your subconscious knows. Most of us live in a continuous subconscious state in which we frequently take action out of intuition. Reality *is*: we in fact are capable of making better choices and being more-so the pilot of our actions, when we are meticulously thinking about them.

#10

I really thought I had you all figured out;

You knew exactly what to do and what to say,

You played me for a fool,

Like a cold hearted serpent you devoured my pride.

I hate you for it.

You were that irritating itch that keeps coming back.

Leaving an unwanted sensation that must be
scratched.

Every time you returned, you tried to deceit me with
your words.

When I finally didn't respond the way you wanted;

You showed your true hideous colours.

Screaming like a psychopath.

Calling me every name that your tiny primitive mind
could think of...

At first I thought your spirit was large and powerful,

But as time passed it dawned on me;

That you are nothing but an itty bitty slimy
cockroach...

#11

My Dearest Grandfather,

Ever since I was a little boy my eyes stared into yours with wild wonder.

I pondered the places you'd been and the things you had seen.

You always remained a mystery to me,

But on one odd day you opened the door to your wisdom and let me have a look of what was inside...

I saw a world filled with passion, love and chaos.

And you said to me;

"Son, the things that you are learning from me of now may appear to be utter nonsense. But knowledge is like fine wine, the longer it ages the stronger it becomes."

And as time goes by, the light begins to shine on your truth.

And for that my faithful grandfather, I will always be in your gratitude,

Because now I can begin to see the curve balls that come my way...

#12

My love for you is deeper than the lowest of canyons,

When I see your sweet tender face, my heart burns
with desire like the blazing heat from a warm cozy
fire.

When I hear your name, my heart sings like the
morning songbirds.

I feel like I'm on a cloud taking me to a land where
sadness and anger ceases to exist,

It is as if I am in a never ending sleep laced with
tranquility and happiness.

I sense a chill go down my spine from the sheer
excitement of your touch.

You make me smile so much that it hurts, but I like
it because I'm hurting over you.

I used to think I knew what love meant. But I was blind,

And now;

I finally understand what love is...

It is a feeling that takes over your entire soul,

Like being possessed,

Possessed by what is not quite a being...

But a feeling.

A feeling that the sun never stops shining, and your heart never stops beating,

You can fly to the stars, and scream from the sky that joy is a sensation everlasting because you are in love.

#13

I sit on the same bench we used to talk on,

The same bench where we shared those special silences and we'd stare into each other's eyes trying to read the other's mind.

I sit on this bench and I take off my glasses, everything is a blur;

Not because of the tears that clog my vision,

But because your face is not smiling into mine.

I don't see the world the same way without you,

Because I'm not looking into your deep brown eyes filled with stars and dreams.

I can't see those dimples that sink into your cheeks

when you smile or laugh at my stupid jokes,

Or hear your voice tell me you care.

So I want to wash that memory away like a stain of blood that poured from my heart, because you don't see in me the same light I see when I look at you.

I stand and rub the tears out my eyes.

Leaving the memories on that bench as I walk away.

#14

The smell of burning wood fills my nose and drifts
into my chest,

I cough intensely at the feeling of my chest tickling
and my eyes wet and irritated.

I smile at the sound of cries in the distance as I know
my end is near, and that's okay!

I know there's no escape from this situation.

The cries get louder and the heat gets stronger,

But still I smile.

#15

My sadness is driving me towards success but away from happiness.

Have you ever looked at your life and couldn't help but notice all the imperfections you so badly want to fix but they are out of your control?

That is my greatest pain, but my greatest reason to have drive.

To live in a life where my opinion isn't frowned upon,

A place where I wouldn't feel like a social reject

and struggle with finding acceptance.

If only I would be able to turn every corner without being afraid of seeing failure on the other side.

To exist in a condition where I can do and say as I
please and nothing holds me back from doing so;

That is what drives me... that is my *true* passion,

I cry because of that empty feeling I get in my heart
when I think too much,

Every day I speak to my father, he tells me things will
get better.

That is all I fight for, that is all I believe in.

Because if things do not, then everything I do after
and in between will all be in vain.

I fight like a madman, trying to resist the urge to give
up,

Like a thousand anchors, pushing me to the floor

waiting for me to give into the struggle.

Day by day I battle against my own discouragement
to give up and let my life tumble apart,

And I am still here and fighting, hoping that one day.

The sun will rise within my soul and I can finally
inhabit a state of harmony...

#16

Love is like a train passing on its way, not caring if
you hop on or not;

It will just keep going whether you want it to or not.
Whether you're in on it or not.

It doesn't care.

Now I sit... And I watch the train do its rounds.

And at every stop I hope to see your face,

But still,

Nothing.

And maybe you'll never show;

You probably won't.

And I may never go anywhere again,

Riding the train of love;

Because I want to ride it with you.

But you don't want to ride it with me.

I just sit here in the station waiting for the train to
pass me by, so I can get a chance to ride it with you.

#17

We are trapped in a vessel,

That inhibits the illusion of individuality.

The illusion of immortality and having purpose.

When reality is that we are nothing but a structure
molded from chemicals,

And that once we deteriorate;

That reality is swept from under our noses,

Before we can even process what just happened.

#18

I want to crumble into your arms;

So you can put me back together.

#19

Laying within the covers of my bed

I feel a sensation of warmth and safety,

But as my eyes go drifting across my room

I fear the monsters that lurk in the shadows.

Not the ones that your parents told you 'don't worry'
about as a child,

But the kind of monsters that reside within our
world.

The ones that we could wake up to tomorrow
morning laughing in our face.

Loss...

Or the reawakening of bad memories...

It could even be the ones that may chase us down the street with their malice intentions at heart.

Such as

Anxiety,

Or death...

But then I ease back in my bed a bit as I think to myself,

The only way not to fear these monsters is to experience every moment;

Second for second,

And then with that the monsters can never chase
you,

And you can share the peace of mind knowing that
your existence is of now and not later.

#20

I feel a cold burning sensation in the depth of my
soul.

As though my very being has been put on ice to
become stagnant and lifeless.

Everyone that comes within radius of me, drives a
feeling of resentment and anger for which I don't
understand;

I don't know what has brought on such a feeling as

I do not care to reconcile my newfound emotion and

I let it grow like a new life within myself.

Making me anew,

To be an individual unbeknownst to myself

For reasons which are completely arbitrary.

Yet simultaneously, I feel a sensation of dread for this new isolated sense of self.

For I don't know if it will equip me with the correct features to face the challenges that are put forth.

I wonder if it is a manifestation of my depression or some other driving force.

#21

The road that I walk down is quiet and melancholy.

There is no such thing as today but only tomorrow;

On that road there is a black cat that crosses me,

It crosses me although this cat has no eyes.

Clouds of grey above me and lightning at my feet,

The pouring rain soaks into my clothes making my
body feel dense and heavy.

I feel the electricity coursing through my veins,
excruciating and violent.

My mind feels numb and I don't know if I can make
it to the end.

My body grows weaker and weaker with each step
and I begin to wonder how long this path goes on...

Just a thought:

Today I had an epiphany.

That we live by the words that others define us by,

But in fact by accepting that as our perception of our
true selves...

We are existing as others and not as ourselves,

But once we are able to accept who we are, and
perceive ourselves as who we *know* we are

We can begin to truly live our lives in the first
person.

Others projected perceptions are meaningless and
are an aspect of their experience of life but not our
own.

Philosophical thought:

Sometimes I wonder if the true meaning of being grounded to reality is to not be grounded at all, and that society has just created an illusionary construct of what we must be. Overtime, that has molded our brains into this false perception of what we share as the true "reality". But in fact, the real reality, is one that we don't even know.

#22

Emotions are a way of making our lives hold meaning.

But without the perception of it,

We are simply

things

and things

upon things

All shifting and drifting in a pool of atoms;

Serving no true purpose

And that we are just *things* that consume and kill *things* in order to create other things.

Just a thought:

Sometimes I wonder why the world hates me so much. It feels as though nothing ever works out in my favor, and I'm always alone and hurting. These days, my heart feels like it's falling apart piece by piece. I get a sick nauseous feeling in my stomach and my chest feels like it's going to pop. I feel so isolated and dissatisfied with my life to the point where some days I ask myself why I'm still even here.

Do I matter?

Will people ever see my good intentions?

Will people ever care?

Will I ever feel like what I do, even matters?

I just want to know why I ask myself, when those I love are going to leave me.

Or should the real question be: when am *I* going to leave them?

I don't know.

I never know until it happens...

Which creates an infinite pending fear that a day will

come when meaningful things and meaningful people go away...

The worst part of it all, is that it always happens at some point.

At some place.

At some time.

Every bit of hope I have feels like it's going to melt away at some point from the heat of my depression and emotional instability.

I just wish people could understand this sensation, as I feel like nobody gets it. So therefore, instead of supporting me, people call me weak and judge and ridicule me.

Can't you see... I fight every day?

Fighting inner demons and chasing that light?! That hope?! Hoping for a better tomorrow? Will it come? They say it comes for all, but I've been waiting 16 years and counting... Where is it? Where the fuck is my relief?

You thought you were the only one, didn't you? Well guess what? I'm a real human being! You reading this, yes *you*... I know what you feel! And maybe I only feel a fraction of what you do, or maybe I feel it tenfold, but I am here to say that you are not alone! We all feel that pain sometimes. That deep, aching, longing, pain. Together, as one, let's change that! Be there for a friend! Tell your family you love them! If we we're all there for one another, we could live in prosperity and happiness. Just asking how someone is feeling could save a life, and you may never know it. Change the world through love, and conquer struggles together! We can make the world a brighter place.

Just a thought:

The only person you should compete with is
yourself.

#23

I feel like a bee trapped in an urban jungle,

With nothing to reap benefit from, but just pollution
in the air and the chaos of a modern construct.

Everything I cling to isn't built for my grip,

I fall weak and sick.

My surroundings keep moving and I feel a strange
sense of difference in how things were before.

#24

There has been a tension rising in my mind;

A tumor with a voice.

It tells me I need to impress and appeal to everyone
in my vicinity,

Reality is that this tumor is deceitful,

It is putting strain on my mind.

It cannot be destroyed,

But it can be molded like clay...

Shaped into something new;

A more positive outlook perhaps.

#25

It doesn't hurt anymore...

Hurt to hear love songs that remind me of you.

It doesn't hurt anymore...

To have the thought of you pass my mind knowing
that you'll never be mine.

Maybe it's just gotten easier because I've faced this
feeling so many times before,

But now when I walk outside,

The sun shines without you there;

And my heart dances to the melodies of life without
you in it.

I feel this peace inside...

Knowing that I didn't make a mistake, but it was in fact, you.

#26

I want to press against you

As the moonlight kisses your neck,

And whisper in your ear that for each star in the sky
is a day I want to spend with you.

#27

Hugs feel like a false promise.

A kind word is the equivalent of a hot breath,

And a smile is merely a sign of passive nature.

Love has no meaning.

Love isn't real.

It's just a show put on for people to watch you,
bemused,

A trick.

A joke.

A lie.

Liars are everywhere...

The funny part is they do it with intuition

And take no notice to the action or the following
ramifications.

It goes unnoticed, unattended,

No love,

No love.

Love is fake,

No love.

Just a thought:

Love... I know I've spoken about it a lot in this book... But I never really strung a true definition to it... So here is my definition of love: Love is about being there for one another, it's about being able to stick by someone's side to the bitter end. Love is about not being afraid to tell someone you care. It's about being able to validate each other's goals and values, and to help them complete them in order to make their life more whole. Love is about being able to admire one another for the smart *and* the stupid things we say. It's about being able to feel comfortable laughing, crying and getting angry together. It's about being able to share every moment good or bad as though it is a full and beautiful one. Love is about being loyal, faithful, and understanding. Love is about being who you are and being comfortable with who you *aren't* around the other. Love is about sharing a story, a legacy together and making it one. Love is unity. Love is passion. Love is desire. Love is changes. Love... Love is a gut feeling. It's something that holds a set definition along with many that are different. Love is confusing. Love can be a discovery. Love is an adventure, it's a journey. It's something to be held close to your heart with complete utter appreciation.

#28

What do you want me to be?

I can be the rays that beam down on you, displaying
a sensation of warmth and comfort following your
every trace.

Or I can be a superhero, always at your side and
ready to save your day.

Tell me what it is, and I'll make it happen;

Do you want me to be your pillow where you can
rest your head when you feel sad and tired?

Or do you want me to be a plane that takes you to
faraway places?

I can be anything you like my love, if you'd just let

me.

Just a thought:

Love is dangerous

True love...

Can drive a man to the brink of insanity.

29

It feels like hot needles piercing all over my skin...

The flood of adrenaline I cannot withstand.

It feels like I'm going to go into overdrive and crash,

Explosions going off in my mind with crimson pools
of blood.

I can feel the tickle of sweat trickling down my face,

I tremble as I clench the blade...

The heat is unbearable as the hot morning sun.

I sit like a ticking time bomb waiting to go off,

But only the future can tell time...

#30

Sinking,

Falling,

Insanity is taking over me.

I don't understand this feeling of confusion and bliss,

I begin to forget why I am here and I start on my
own venture.

The sky begins to watch me,

The ground begins to follow me,

The air begins to smell me,

And I can't say I don't like it;

Because when things make no sense it's more interesting.

I'm getting lost in this world and it's full of crazy joy rides that seem to make no sense.

Who gives a fuck?

I'm headed somewhere, aren't I?

Isn't that all that matters?

#31

Taste my tears and tell me if their good,

Because it's a meal you made for yourself,

A grave you laid in the ground with our love written
on it.

Was it worth it?

Worth it to deceive me, and make me think that you
were worth my time?

You didn't have to do this to us, you know?

You didn't have to end it the way you did...

#32

I try to make others happy,

But even if it is a success I still feel as if I failed...

Even if the sky is bright and blue,

All I see is clouds of grey.

I feel lost...

Lost, like a tumbleweed blowing in the wind not
knowing where it's going to land.

My heart feels hollow like an oak tree with nothing
inside but black cob webs.

Those who are there, aren't really there...

I feel lost...

I feel pain.

I hurt like a wounded animal, dying slowly with its life oozing from where it's injured, distorted with no one there for comfort...

Waiting for it to end...

I am stuck in a pool of black, slowly drowning with no view of shore.

I sit in open waters slowly choking back what consumes me to the point where it overtakes me. I stop fighting it and let the waves drag me to my demise...

I

Am

So

Lost...

#33

I feel eyes of hatred and judgement everywhere I go

Stabbing my conscious like knives.

There's nowhere I can run or hide to escape them

It's a never ending pain;

It's the type of pain that consumes you,

The type of pain that will drive you to the point of insanity.

The type of pain that leaves you in a hot sweat wondering where and who you are.

It makes you want to cry, but you know it is only a sign of weakness.

It itches like a scab,

You know that if you try to fight back it will only
make it worse.

All you can do is sit,

Sit and let it slowly eat you whole...

Just a thought:

Loneliness is an illusion of the mind. For when we are able to find comfort in our own solitude, we are accompanied by contentment.

#34

As I lie on the cold wooden floor I stare at the stars
that are sprinkled across the sky.

I feel this cold emptiness inside but the fire warms
me with a blanket of solace;

The moon has a warm tender glow that puts me into
a trance of infatuation,

For the beauty it holds is like no other.

Every night it puts me to sleep and helps me forget
the pain that I've been through,

Only for me to wait all day the next day,

To fall in love with the night sky again.

Okay, so you've reached the end, I truly hope that it started some sort of spark in your mind, or your heart; if it was just entertaining that's okay too! I am just glad to share my thoughts and my message, my goal is to inspire and try to make some sort of a change in the world big or small. Now, I know I am no Buddha or Mahatma Ghandi, but I am a person who has grown, and changed what I choose to define my life, more times than I can count. But with change comes experience, and from that comes the birth of knowledge. Now this story is yours too! It's your experience as well, so what comes next, is what you make out of it...

Made in the USA
San Bernardino, CA
09 November 2018